JO,

enjoy!

Best wishes

Louise
xxx

1

Lessons in Pug

ISBN: 979-8-628783-0-0-9

Lessons

in

Pug

How one crazy pup changed my life

By Louise Green

At first glance you may think this is merely a book about a dog. You may also think it is about the clueless owner who has no idea what she is doing.

You would be right on both counts.

But it is also a book about energy, love and transformation.

Oh, and fear. Buckets full of the stuff. I have faced it head on and I haven't always won but there have been more victories than defeats.

There will always be a reason to put something off and to let that fear win. For a while, I allowed that to become my truth and this book nearly never made it. Comparison has been a worthy adversary and perfection has been my excuse to procrastinate.

And then I remembered who the hell I am. Putting your words and thoughts out into the world is both terrifying and liberating in equal measure and something I have wanted for so long.

So, fear, do your worst, because I did it anyway.

Introduction Part One

Lessons in Pug

The definition of success is as individual as the person that achieves it. For some, it may be dedicating their lives to inspiring and helping others. Whilst self-made millionaires acquire phenomenal wealth that most of us can only dream of. World-class athletes devote their lives to becoming the best in their chosen sport. Award-winning actors and musicians fill our world with incredible stories and beautiful music.

This story is *my* success. It is about me, my dog and our life together. Maybe not extraordinary, but special nonetheless.

I am a 50-year-old Wife and Grandmother and it has always been my dream to write a book, ever since I had an article published in the local paper, aged 11. There was something about seeing my name in print that was magical to me.

So, here it is.

I do so hope you enjoy it.

Introduction Part Two

One of the many things that I have learned on this journey is the tremendous amount of animal charities out there that are working tirelessly to rescue and re-home unwanted and sometimes mistreated pets.

One woman's story really touched my heart. Rebecca Drake, otherwise known as Bubblebecca Pugs, has dedicated her life to rescuing pugs from all over the world. Her endless commitment to these beautiful dogs is inspirational in itself. Alongside this, her tireless mission to care for as many pugs as she can and give them the life they deserve, filled with love and affection, is such an incredible story that I knew I had to help.

Cue, my little book. For every copy that is sold, I will happily and lovingly donate 50% of the profits to Rebecca and her gorgeous grumble. For more information on Bubblebecca and her amazing rescue mission, please visit www.bubblebecca.co.uk or follow her on Facebook, Instagram and Twitter. Another way to support her cause is to take a look at the Amazon wish list;

https://www.amazon.co.uk/registry/wishlist/JEAFZT1X W6AI/ref=cm_sw_r_cp_ep_ws_90.LAbSZWH3YW

Dad,

This is for you. I finally did it.

XXX

Chapters

Chapter One

Man's Best Friend

As I share my story with you, it will hopefully become apparent why becoming a dog owner was such a huge deal for me. I also hope it will make you smile. I promise you that everything is true and a completely honest, warts-and all account of my experiences.

For most of you reading this, you will have grown up having a dog, or some other pet in your life. You may have formed a close bond with your four-legged friend and have gone on to become a dog owner as an adult and probably never given it a second thought.

My childhood was somewhat different to most of the kids I grew up with. My parents were significantly older and their beliefs and opinions often reflected that. Sadly, they would not or could not allow themselves to change their way of thinking.

This resulted in a somewhat rigid existence, full of rules that made little sense to a child. One such rule was no pets of any kind. It was non-negotiable. Animals had no place in the home. They were dirty, smelly and destructive creatures and my Mother, in particular, viewed any pet owner as someone beneath her, and the homes that they lived in as squalid. This sweeping generalisation included all pets, even the humble goldfish. There was however, one animal in particular that my Mother had a real problem with. DOGS.

I was raised to believe dogs were animals to fear. They could not be trusted and could 'go on the turn' at any moment, meaning you could quite literally be mauled to death. Larger breeds were the ones to be most afraid of, although the small ones were vicious and would sink their teeth into you and hang off your limbs. Jack Russells were one of the main culprits that my Mother had a particular hatred for. As if that wasn't enough to burden a child with, I was also brainwashed into believing that a German Shepherd was not a mere dog. A German Shepherd was the most evil, powerful, child eating machine that would literally tear me limb from limb if I so much as looked at it. I encountered a lot of German Shepherds in my childhood. I would hold my breath, squeeze my hands tight and cross the road as quickly as I could. Although I knew I must not run because this would cause the dog to give chase and I would not be able to outrun it. I literally lived in terror, constantly dreading the next encounter.

I will never forget my Mother complaining when she spotted a dog in the street. It was as if they came out on purpose just to annoy her. She would glare at the owners and make a performance out of avoiding the 'beast', sometimes even dragging me into the road just to escape a Poodle. These encounters would shape the rest of the day as she would relive it, numerous times.

Watching television would further fuel the irrational beliefs and fears growing inside of me. It seemed as if every TV villain had a huge, vicious dog, as its sidekick. My Mother would curse under her breath and yell at me not to look at it. With this constant reinforcement, I could do nothing but believe all that I was being told. I had nothing to compare it to, or anyone else's point of view to consider, although this would, no doubt have been an exercise in futility as my Mother's beliefs were so strong. There simply was no such thing as a well-behaved, gentle dog.

I realise now that it was her warped way of dealing with her own fear and attempting to keep me safe. No doubt she had been raised with these beliefs. It is sad to think that she never learned to overcome it as it really did affect her day-to-day life.

Visiting relatives as a child was nothing short of miserable if they dared have a dog in their home. The car journey to their house usually centred on the topic of the dog and 'whether it had been put outside.' Then, as we arrived and could hear the dog barking, my Mother's mood would rapidly deteriorate. The tension was almost too much to bear as we walked in and were met with a boisterous, over-excited dog that was jumping up at us. I was crippled with fear as we sat down and I could not take my eyes of it, too scared to move an inch in case it went for me. Of course, the dog could sense exactly how I was feeling and become unsettled and this would usually lead it to be banished to another room for terrifying me. And once again, it served as further proof that my Mother was right.

Adult life was a whole other challenge. I found myself hiding my fears and withdrawing from situations which may involve an encounter with a canine. I missed out on many conversations and potential friendships. It did not matter how nice a person was, or how well we got on, if they had a dog, I could not have them in my life. I was as judgemental of them as my Mother before me and I felt resigned to my fate. Unconsciously, I developed a blasé attitude as a front to cover up how I truly felt. So what if others didn't understand? At least I would be safe. Looking back, I had no idea how much this influenced the choices I made. I was very sad and very lonely for a long time.

I honestly did not feel as if I had missed out though and I accepted this way of life. However, once I got married and our children arrived, the subject of a family pet reared its ugly head. My Husband knew how I felt so it was no surprise to him that I was against it from the very start. It was beyond comprehension to me that our family would benefit from having any pet, let alone a canine. No amount of reasoning was ever going to convince me. I would be too afraid to be in my own home with it. I promise you that I am not exaggerating. The topic was closed. No dogs, ever.

Chapter Two

Little Baby Pug

Fast forward to 2008.

My daughter, Michaela (Kayla), was 14 years old. Like any typical teenager, she went from one fad to another in the blink of an eye. Be it a boy band, a magazine, a 'must have' item of clothing or a TV show. Until, that is, she discovered Pugs.

I do not remember what had initially sparked her interest in this particular breed but it wasn't long before the interest grew into a desire and eventually into what can only be described as an obsession. A couple of her school friends had recently gotten dogs, but they were much larger breeds. One was, of course, a German Shepherd. We did not know anyone who owned a Pug. It is true to say that, at the time, the breed was growing in popularity and some celebrities were snapped with Pugs of their own, but even so, her fixation was baffling to us. She began to look online at pictures and selling sites and shouting out 'LITTLE BABY PUG,' every time one popped up on the screen. They all looked the same to me, but she would point out that this one had a curlier tail, or this one was a slightly different colour, but they were all perfect in her eyes. She soon began to create stories around this imaginary pet. She called him Eddie and no matter where we were or what we were up to, she would always remind us that if Eddie was with us, he would be snuggled up on the sofa, or running around the park, or sitting on the back seat of the car with her. He would, of course, behave impeccably, doing exactly what she told him to do and they would both be living their best life together. I made my feelings perfectly clear on the subject although this did nothing to deter her.

Despite my misgivings, we had owned a rabbit some years earlier. We bought him for my son's birthday and as cute as he was, with his long floppy ears and twitchy nose, I never formed any sort of attachment to him. He would hop over to me whilst I was hanging out the washing and pee all over my feet. The children all adored him but I never saw him as anything other than an inconvenience and another thing to have to think about. We went on to own another rabbit a few years later, which we bought for Michaela. We called her Boo. We had hopes of her becoming a house bunny, (maybe if she had, none of this would have ever happened), but she chewed through every cable in the house. Toilet training proved impossible and stressed me out as I was constantly on edge, waiting for the next accident. Whilst she never peed on my feet, I had little to do with her. It was nice to watch her hopping around the garden but that was the extent of my feelings.

I was grateful that my sons did not jump on the Pug Bandwagon. They too assumed that this was another fad and knowing my beliefs, never imagined any other outcome. Life was fairly hectic at that time. With three teenagers and both of us working full time, there was always a lot going on. Even if we had *wanted* to get a dog, there was no spare time, not to mention the responsibility, the expense, the work and the POO. There was more than enough of an argument to say no, irrespective of how I felt.

The weeks and months passed and still she continued in her quest. I had never seen her so single-minded about anything. Her drive and determination were a real credit to her, particularly as up until that point, she had always been more than happy to let the world go by and live in her own bubble. I remember thinking that I wished she was this focused on her school work! I had certainly underestimated her. She created a folder, packed full of information about the breed. It was a Pug-a-pedia with everything anyone could possibly want to know. Assuming that is, that you were actually looking for one. And so it continued, night after night. Eddie this and Eddie that. Pug this and Pug that. Being the youngest, we would often cut Michaela more slack (there, boys, I said it) and we allowed this fantasy to grow and gain momentum.

There *must* have been a series of events that took place over the following weeks, but for the life of me I do not know what they were. I slowly began shifting my outlook from outright rejection at the whole notion of owning a dog, to finding my thoughts being consumed by curly tails and squishy faces (not a huge surprise given the months of brainwashing). I do remember telling myself this was so much easier than battling with my daughter and I held the faint hope that it may now fizzle out if I feigned interest.

I am laughing to myself that I could have been that gullible.

I began to ask more and more questions. She had the answer to any objection that I raised. That is, except the price. £1000, £1500, £2000 and beyond.

FOR A DOG?

Even though we weren't *actually* looking, that was a staggering amount of money. We could do an awful lot with that sort of cash. Other breeds were nowhere near as expensive. Another shocking realisation was that not all the ads were what they appeared to be. It soon became clear that there were many expensive scams in place to tug at your heart strings and convince you to hand over your cash for a dog that did not actually exist. There were hundreds for sale, up and down the country and they were selling fast. I found myself thinking that, with their round bellies and squishy faces, that they were kind of cute. That is not to say that we were getting one. It was purely a way to engage with my daughter on a subject that she clearly loved. Or so I told myself.

Then the inevitable happened. One evening in late July I turned to my husband, Michael and said, "Let's do it. Let's go and buy a Pug." Michaela had no idea.

Chapter Three

The Day an Angel came to Stay

Early the next morning, while the kids were still in bed, we set off. We had found a kennels on the internet in Lincolnshire that had 7/8th Pug puppies for sale. We had no idea what the other 1/8th was, or what this meant in terms of 'pugness'. The few pics on the website showed puggy-looking pugs and that was good enough for us. To be honest with you, the price was much more affordable compared to so many other ads and so, just like that, the decision was made. As it turned out, the mix was a good one as he was less 'squishy' and therefore did not suffer with breathing problems that are common amongst the breed.

I could hardly contain my excitement when we arrived. I had no idea what to expect, all I could think about was getting our 'Eddie' home. We were greeted by a somewhat grumpy man, who looked bored, or uninterested at our arrival. I mumbled an incoherent sentence about wanting a puppy, suddenly feeling out of my depth and thinking it was a very bad idea. He asked if we had reserved one. I felt a sudden surge of panic in my stomach. What? I looked at Michael and we both stared back at him blankly. I hadn't even considered that there would be no puppies available and I certainly did not know that I could have reserved one.

The man mumbled under his breath and began walking away from us. We took his half-hearted wave as an indication that we should follow him. We were taken to one of a number of large concrete pens. It was filled with puppies, all excitedly barking and fighting for our attention. It was quite a sight. In an instant, I saw him. He was jumping higher than all the other pups, (that should have been a clue right there) and in that split second I knew he was coming home with us. Someone reached over, picked him up and handed him over to me and just like that I had a crazy wriggling ball of fur in my arms, licking my face and biting my clothes.

Minutes later we were on our way home. We were not vetted at all and we didn't ask any questions. When I look back on this, it still shocks me. We knew nothing about this dog, but we honestly never gave it a second thought. I had taken longer to decide what to eat for lunch than whether this tiny puppy and all of his needs was right for our family.

We had (had) enough foresight to purchase a crate though, en route to the kennels, so very gingerly, we placed him in it and began our journey home. I sat on the back seat next to him. We stared at each other for the longest time. It hadn't sunk in what we had just done. All I could think about was getting home and seeing Michaela's face.

There was no question that he was incredibly cute, with huge brown eyes, large floppy ears and soft fawn fur. He was so small that he fitted across the width of the crate with room to spare. I gently stroked him and he laid down on his new doggy blanket. We had also bought him a toy – a blue fluffy, squeaky bone which I nudged under his nose. I was expecting a sniff, or a wag of his tail. Nothing. I was ever so slightly miffed. I mean, here we were, getting up at the crack of dawn and driving for hours to give this pup a new home. The very least he could do was pretend to be grateful. I made myself comfy and started to plan our big reveal to the children when we eventually got home.

Moments later, the puppy was on his feet and he began moving his tiny head back and forth. I shot up, sensing this was not a good sign even though I did not know exactly what was wrong with him. He looked increasingly uncomfortable and as I contemplated getting him out of the crate he made a pathetic retching noise and I looked on in horror as he began to vomit. Not just a bit. It reached all four corners of his crate and his blue fluffy bone was now a disgusting brown lump of mush. I screamed out to Michael for help. He was shouting instructions to me from the driver's seat. The puppy looked at me as if to say, "Well, do something!" So

I cleaned him up as best I could and with a bag of vomit-filled dog blankets at my feet, we settled down once again.

All of the excitement must have worn him out because he was soon fast asleep, so I continued planning our big surprise. I wanted it to be perfect, but I had no idea how I was going to sneak in without the puppy being seen. We were going to have be out of the car as quickly as possible, before any of the children got up to open the front door. Never had a car journey taken so long.

As we pulled up on the drive I was feeling somewhere between nauseous, excited, hysterical, and absolutely terrified. There were so many thoughts running round and round in my head and I wasn't able to concentrate on a single one of them,

"QUICK!" I shouted to Michael as he wrestled the puppy out of the car. I was standing guard, poised to intercept anyone. Looking back, I don't know why I was so concerned, the children never normally bothered to get up and open the door and today was no exception. Michael placed the puppy in my arms and led me silently into the kitchen. As expected, the children were all watching TV and paid no attention to our arrival.

I stayed at one end of the kitchen, where I was hidden from view and called out to Michaela to come in, all the time struggling to keep the wriggling ball of fur in my arms. I was thankful, that for once, she came straight away. Walking into the kitchen, she looked over at me and then looked down at the puppy.

"We got him," I said, barely able to speak. It took a second for this to sink in. Her eyes were glued on him. Silence. Time stood still. Then she screamed. She ran over to me and began to cry as I handed over the little baby pug that she had dreamed about for so long. The boys came running in to see what all the noise was about. Cue more screams.

The next few minutes were just a total joy to behold. Excitement, chatter, laughter and an overwhelming feeling of love. The puppy was eager to get down and examine his new surroundings. Once on the floor, where we could all get a better look at him, there was a collective "Awwwwwww" as he took his first tentative steps. There were so many questions as we watched him trot about. Everyone was talking at once as the puppy started sniffing the rug. He then began circling, which was of no significance to us as novice dog owners until he then squatted down in front of us and did a giant sh*t. We all watched on before realising we had to do something.

"Take him outside," someone shouted.

"It's a bit late for that," I responded. "Did we get any poo bags? Where are they? Can someone get some wipes? Hurry up!!" Everyone sprang into action. Michaela picked him up and carried him at arm's length to the garden whilst we got on with cleaning up the mess.

Once we had recovered, the conversation turned to his name.

"He doesn't look like an Eddie," said Michaela. And soon everyone began giving their suggestions on what he should be called. I could make very little sense of any of it so I just sat back whilst they carried on the debate. I glanced up at the TV that was still playing. It was one of their favourite shows, 'Charmed'. As I carried on watching, the Angel, Leo appeared on the screen. I got goose bumps.

"LEO!!!" I shouted above all the chatter. They all fell silent and looked at me and then at the TV. And that, as they say, was that. Our puppy, Leo, was named after an Angel. I hope you can appreciate the irony.

Unable to cook a proper meal with a puppy in the house, we sat in the kitchen, tucking into pizza, trying to eat it as fast as possible so we could get back to the fur ball that was laying in his crate just a few feet away.

Maybe two whole minutes passed and then little Leo decided to complain. Not a lot, just a bit of a whinge. Our pizzas flew up in the air as we all rushed over to him. Of course, he was fine. He just needed some alone time. He needed to adjust to his new life with all of the excited humans around him. So what did we do? We picked him up and took him into the kitchen with us, smothering him in kisses and talking in baby voices in an attempt to reassure him. I ate the rest of my pizza with him asleep on my lap. We didn't take our eyes off him.

And so it began. A catalogue of mistakes and a rollercoaster ride of tears and laughter, borne out of an incredible love for this dog.

That is the day an angel came to stay and my life changed forever.

Chapter Four

First Days

I can only compare the first few days with Leo the puppy to bringing a new born baby into your home for the first time. Only worse. Much, much worse.

A lack of sleep, a whole lot of poo, biting, vomit, scratching, chasing, still more poo, shouting and overall chaos. At least with a baby, you can put it in a cot and you know that it won't go anywhere. With a puppy, you do not have this luxury, (well, we did, but we just didn't want to put him in his crate). We learned very quickly to close all the doors and block all the holes in the fence that we had previously never known existed.

We had a stream of eager visitors at our door. Squeals and screams and laughter filled our home as people witnessed the total bundle of cuteness that we now owned. Leo loved the attention of course, and he was just passed from one pair of arms to another. He was simply irresistible and boy, did he know it. All the fuss just reinforced his behaviour, I see that now. I still wouldn't change a single second.

The sound of his tiny paws on the kitchen floor was, for me, one of the cutest sounds. He was still a bit like 'Bambi on Ice' and he often tried to run but couldn't get his grip, so despite his best efforts, he very often didn't get anywhere, resembling a cartoon character. I remember that he would just hang off my dressing gown and literally swing on it whilst I tried to hang out the washing. (Still, at least he wasn't peeing on my foot). He got stuck behind a gap in the shed, constantly. He wanted anything and everything and demanded our attention at all times, which, of course we gave him.

He had every dog toy that we could find; three dog beds, blankets, chews and total, unconditional love. He had us all wrapped around his furry paws and there wasn't a thing we could do about it.

I had to go to work the very next day but rang home at every available opportunity for an update of what he was doing, if he had eaten, where he was at that precise second when I called. I also revelled in the attention from my work colleagues as I had now joined the club by becoming a dog owner. Everyone wanted to know about him and I felt as if I now had the approval of many that I had previously had little dealings with in. I definitely felt like a proud parent.

Conversely, those closest to me reacted with utter disbelief and who could blame them? I hardly believed it myself.

"BUT YOU HATE DOGS," they repeated over and over, shocked at my decision. I had no words. I had no valid, tangible reason for this change of heart. I just became a dog owner overnight and had absolutely no idea what I had done. I was too busy basking in the glow of having a cute puppy in my house and finally, after decades out in the cold, I was part of 'the gang'.

The next few weeks passed in a blur as our routine became dominated by toilet training, and attempting to function within our everyday lives whilst taking care of the puppy. Every thought we had was influenced by him. Who was going to let him out? Who was going to take him to the vets for his check up? Is he eating enough? Is he warm enough? Is he going to feel lonely when we are all out? We left the radio on, just to make ourselves feel better.

Leaving the house was nothing short of a military operation, ensuring all doors were properly closed and anything that he could destroy was out of reach. Countless visits to the garden just to be sure he couldn't squeeze out a little drop or two before we left. An extra blanket, an extra toy, an extra treat. Endless goodbye cuddles and kisses. We did not want to leave him, even for a second.

We all rushed to get home and see his squishy face and crazy, curly tail. We screamed and sang and ran around the house with him, encouraging his already excited behaviour. He would run round and round in circles, snorting and panting. He would jump up constantly and although our voices said no, our actions and energy were telling him a different story.

Leo was not old enough to go for a walk just yet, so had endless energy to burn off and our evenings soon turned into games of ball throwing and hide and seek until one of us fell asleep. No prizes for guessing who was asleep first. We were all exhausted. It was only, temporary though, because once we could take him out into the big wide world, he would be so worn out that he would spend the rest of his day asleep in his bed. Of course, this was complete rubbish, I know that now. Let me tell you it has taken 10 years for this to happen and even now he still has bouts of craziness and unpredictable behaviour. When people meet him for the first time they cannot believe his age as he is still as boisterous as a pup.

We have gone through so many changes since we first got Leo. The children have all grown up and left home. When Michaela moved out I could not bear the thought of Leo going as well, so he has stayed with us. We have moved house and jobs, had holidays and done all of the things that families do and Leo was at the heart of it all. If he was going to be left too long, we wouldn't go out. If someone wasn't able to stay with him, we would cancel our plans. If the holiday cottage wasn't dog friendly, we didn't book it (and as for holidays abroad, you'll will have to keep reading to find out all about that).

In a nutshell, the student had become the master, or in our case, the Pug had become the Pack Leader.

Chapter Five

People

Earlier, I touched on being withdrawn from friendships. Not wanting to expose my weaknesses, I kept myself to myself for the majority of my life. So, when Leo was old enough to be taken out into the big wide world, I was ill-equipped to deal with the amount of attention a pug puppy and his owner would get.

Complete strangers would just stop in their tracks and squeal 'Oh, you have a Pug PUPPY!!' and they would come hurtling over to me as if this was a reason to invade my personal space and start petting my dog. They would chat to me like they had known me for years whilst I stood there dumbstruck, filled with horror that this was considered acceptable behaviour. Grown women were reduced to jabbering wrecks, talking in baby language to my dog and kissing him.

I remember one occasion when I took him out, a car screeched to a halt next to me and the passenger door flew open. There was what can only be described as a hysterical woman fighting with her seat belt.

'PUG!!' She screamed. 'I have to come and see it,' I was speechless whilst this crazy woman slobbered all over my dog and proceeded to tell me her life story and how much she loved the breed and she had several of her own and they were now on the way to the vet with one, but she just had to stop and say hello. And as quickly as she arrived, she was back in the car and waving goodbye as the car sped off.

There was some kind of unspoken law that I was not aware of that meant if you had a dog, any Tom, Dick or Harry could just come up to you and start talking to you. A bit like when you are pregnant and people want to touch your bump. Only worse, much worse. People would tell you horrific stories of when their dog died and how they are still grieving. I met one dog owner who was convinced that Leo was his late Pug that had been reincarnated and would only call him by his dead dog's name.

Neighbours that I had nodded to for years and years would suddenly find a reason to talk to me. I had walked past their front gardens on the school run with a baby in a pram and they didn't so much as bat an eyelid. But a puppy? Well, let's make conversation with this woman.

I was not prepared for this side effect of dog ownership. I really struggled with it and, to my everlasting shame, I began to withdraw from dog walking duties as the thought of this interaction quite frankly terrified me. I began to dread the very thought of taking him out and I would imagine scenarios that almost always came to fruition. Leo got his lead tangled up around another owner's ankles, jumped on a mobility scooter and cocked his leg, or jumped up uncontrollably when someone came over to say hello to him. It is something that I regret, but I knew that my stress was not the best for him and in many cases, causing the behaviour I was dreading. My husband took over the bulk of the dog walking and this was much, much better. He is a much more calm and sociable person and he enjoyed the interactions.

I am very pleased to say that over time, I gained confidence, I read books on dog behaviour and gradually I joined in the dog walking duties once again. I now often find myself approaching almost any dog I see, particularly Pugs. Definitely not German Shepherds – I don't think I will ever lose that fear that is inherent in me. But there I am, going up to dog owners that I do not know and talking to their dogs. Even writing this now, it seems such a huge thing for me to do. I cannot now ever imagine my life now without a dog.

Chapter Six

Dog Training

I have made no secret that we had absolutely no idea what we were doing and although we all absolutely adored Leo, our lives were total chaos and revolved completely around him. It was time to consult a professional.

We had had a wealth of advice from other dog owners, most of which was conflicting. Someone suggested that I buy some small metal discs that I could hurl at him every time he did something wrong. Another recommendation was to squirt water at him to stop unwanted behaviour and we did try it, for about an hour. He was drenched, the sofa that he wasn't allowed on was drenched, the carpets all over the house where he ran excitedly were covered in wet paw prints and my kitchen floor looked like it had flooded. It was time to take action.

We decided that puppy classes would be a good idea. 'Teach your dog some manners. Train them to walk on the lead. Take back control.' They promised so much and sounded exactly what we needed. Turns out no-one else in Suffolk knew what they were doing with their dogs either because every class was fully booked with waiting lists. We didn't really have time to wait. He was already running our lives, at least that what I thought. I realise now that it was us, mainly me, that was encouraging this bad behaviour and I would give in to those puppy eyes in a heartbeat. If I had persevered and stayed consistent, life would have been much easier and calmer for everyone, including Leo.

And then, one Friday evening, the local free newspaper dropped onto the door mat. Leo was up in a nano-second, barking, jumping and running in circles. "Why??" I ask him as I got up to get the paper. I never usually looked at it, but I casually scanned through it whilst keeping one eye on Leo and willing him to calm down. It was then I saw it – an ad for puppy training classes! In a somewhat ironic twist, it was at a German Shepherd training club. They were opening their doors to pups for an hour before the all the 'proper' dogs arrived. Whilst the thought of encountering my nemesis filled me with fear, I was desperate. The trainer sounded very knowledgeable when I spoke to her on the phone so I booked him in. On the day of the first lesson Michael, Michaela and I set off. I was apprehensive and had no idea what to expect but, honestly, how bad could it be?

For training purposes, only one person was permitted to be with the puppy whilst the other family members could observe from the other end of the hall. So Michael and Michaela took their seats with the growing audience whilst I was taking one for the team on the front line of puppy training.

Let's just say that Leo wasn't a star pupil. He had the wrong collar, he had the wrong lead. He jumped up continuously. He *bit* the instructor and to my complete horror she grabbed hold of him and pushed him down to the floor and called him a 'Little Sh*t'. I don't know who was more terrified – me or the dog. That was the first five minutes of registration.

It didn't improve. In fact, it got a whole lot worse.

He sat in the wrong place. He paid absolutely no attention to my commands. He jumped, constantly. The other puppies sat, slept or judged whilst Leo, pulled on his lead, bit me numerous times and stressed me out more than I can tell you. I could see the instructor was getting frustrated with us. I'm fairly sure that no-one else could hear a word she was saying because my voice filled the hall with pointless pleading for him to 'sit, stay, stop, LEO!'

We started with the basic sit command which we had been practising at home so I was ok with this and had plenty of treats on hand. I looked over to Michael and Michaela who gave me an encouraging thumbs up. I did feel a moment of smugness, knowing that this was a good decision on my part.

We then progressed to using props – a gate to be precise. My mission, should I choose to accept it, was to get through said gate before Leo. Not only that but he had to sit still and watch me and wait for me to call him over to me. I actually burst out laughing but quickly stifled it as the Instructor caught my eye. I mean, it didn't *sound* that difficult, in principle. In fact, it sounded perfectly reasonable. I looked around me as the other dog owners were making it look as effortless as breathing. I just had no idea how to do it. Needless to say, it was a race to the finish. No matter how slowly or sneakily I nudged that bloody gate, he was, apparently, possessed with some sort of ninja superpower and squeezed himself through the narrowest gap and was off to go and tell Michael and Michaela what a good boy he was.

"Now you are going to command your dogs to lie down. Get them into the sit position, and move the treat down to the floor and your dog will follow. Use the command DOWN." Knowing that this was unlikely, I prayed that this was the last task for the evening. Leo was sitting at my feet, with his eye on the tasty treat. His eyes followed my hand to the floor. His bum remained up in the air. He just would not lie down. He looked at me as if I was the stupid one. The trainer sighed as she watched me and walked over. She stood in front of him with a look of contempt on her face. She raised her arm and pointed to the ground in a somewhat dramatic gesture.

'DOWN!' she yelled. Nothing. Leo just looked up at her, panting. She tried again, 'DOWN!' He stood up. She looked at me with the same look and walked away from us to a much more obedient pooch. I was mortified.

And so, to the final task of the evening. We were to perform a recall and to this day I am sure she was determined to get her own back as she announced that Leo was up first.

So there I stood, in front of an audience of somewhat judgemental dog owners. (At least, I had decided they were judgemental. They could, in truth, have been very nice people).

So Leo was taken to the opposite end of the hall. The trainer was holding on tight to his collar as he struggled and strained almost choking himself in an attempt to get free. All I had to do was get him to run to me by being the most exciting and enticing thing in the place. He then had to sit in front of me whilst I calmly stepped forward and attached his lead. I can hear you laughing already. This is how it went down.

I called, jumped, waved my arms and all but begged this puppy to come to me. His little cartoon character legs were galloping on the spot. My voice grew louder as she let him go and he started running towards me. All the time I was thinking, 'I am going to prove you wrong. I can do this. I can control this crazy bundle of fur.'

Leo had me in his sights as I continued to jump up and down, my voice getting higher and higher and sounding more and more desperate. He was almost at my feet. Stop! I was thinking to myself. Wait. He ran behind me.

I could hear the frustration in the trainer's voice as she barked 'Get him to come back and sit in front of you.' Like it was that easy.

He started to come back. Ok, I've got this. Then he took off in the opposite direction. I ignored the sniggers and continued to call him. Clearly loving all of the attention, Leo ran around and around, grinning and wagging his tail. My calls were diminishing. I was losing hope. I felt pathetic as I had no clue how to get my dog on the bloody lead. I was tempted to just start chasing him around the room but that is what they were all expecting. I stood firm, confident that I could turn this around. Then the ultimate humiliation.

Leo paused for a moment and looked right at me. With renewed hope, I began waving my arms and calling him, louder than ever. He ran towards me and just before he reached my feet, he circled then squatted and did one of his trademark giant sh*ts in the middle of the floor. Silence. Someone handed me a mop and bucket whilst Leo did a lap of honour.

We took our seats, at the back of the hall as the other owners performed perfect recall after perfect recall. Leo was oblivious to what had just occurred, and despite his energetic performance was still jumping about.

As we walked out of the hall, we had to pass the German Shepherds waiting to come in. It was as if they too were judging us, sneering at my little dog and sneering at me as a hopeless dog owner. I felt sure that one of them was going to eat Leo, or me, or both. I could see them breaking free from the heavy duty chain leads and coming to kill us.

We continued this humiliation for 3 more weeks and each session ended the same. I would spend all day dreading it, worrying about what he was going to do next and what new ways he would find to humiliate me. I realise now that I was creating a self-fulfilling prophecy and Leo was simply feeding off my energy. We decided that our boy was just a bit more special than others and we would just have to learn to live with it.

In hindsight, I wish I had persevered and found another class that was more suited to our particular needs, but I assumed they were all the same and quite honestly, I was just relieved it was over.

Chapter Seven

Lost

A regular Monday evening turned into a night I shall never forget.

Michaela had taken Leo out for a walk whilst the rest of us stayed at home. It was unusual for us all to be in the house at the same time and I am so very grateful that we were. She had only been gone a few minutes when my phone rang. My first thought was she has probably forgotten poo bags, even though I reminded her before she left. Nothing could have prepared me for what she said. "I have lost Leo." She murmured. Her voice was trembling. My heart began pounding as the words sank in. I remember screaming down the phone and shouting to Michael and the boys.

"HOW?" I demanded to know. She had been looking at her phone and had failed to notice when he somehow managed to slip off the lead and by the time she realised, he had vanished.

The next hour of our lives were a blur. Michael and the boys were dispatched in their cars to patrol the area whilst I pursued on foot to look for him in all the places a car could not get to. I ran to the park where Michaela was working her way through the bushes, calling out his name. I told her to stay around there and I would look elsewhere although I did not know which direction to take. He could be absolutely anywhere. I started to run. I shouted out his name, becoming more and more frantic with every second that passed. I ran into gardens, down alleys, behind shops. Nothing.

'Where are you?' I yelled at the top of my voice. I looked in bushes, in ditches and stopped every single person that I saw, most of whom viewed me with some apprehension. I was tear-stained, breathless and gabbling like a mad woman. No one had seen him. I imagined all sorts. Dog nappers throwing him into a sack in the back of a white van, a hit-and-run driver leaving him fighting for his life at the roadside or trapped in a ditch with only minutes of oxygen. You get the idea.

I called Michael. No luck. I was sobbing, thinking about life without him. Thinking that he could be frightened and hurt and not understand why we weren't there for him. My mind was in full-scale overdrive. I stood in the street feeling overwhelmed by the situation and completely powerless. I didn't know what else to do. I walked across the park one final time, praying he would come bounding out of a bush. He didn't.

With a heavy heart, still sobbing, I turned to make my way home. I wanted to stay right there, for the rest of the night, but deep down I knew it was pointless. I needed a miracle. The thought of losing him was too painful to bear. I chose to block this out and instead decided to feel numb, purposefully not focusing on anything. Not daring to think that he might be gone forever. It just didn't seem real.

As I looked up to cross the road to my house I saw her. An angel. On my doorstep was a woman I did not know. She was bent down, holding on to Leo who was jumping up at her uncontrollably. I screamed, waved, shouted as the poor woman tried to calm me down as well and get me across the road without getting run over.

I sobbed uncontrollably as she told me that she had found him in a bush in the park and had left her own dog with a friend so she could use the lead to bring him back home. Thank goodness we had (had) his name tag made so she knew where to bring him.

I wanted to hug her. I was babbling incoherently and I think she soon realised there was little point in trying to calm me down. I thanked her for the thousandth time as she left and opened the front door to let us in. I sat on the floor in our hall whilst a hyped up Leo jumped all over me. I rang everyone to call off the search and get them back home with us.

I think we all learned just how much a part of our family he had become and we never wanted

to go through that again. I felt so incredibly lucky.
It changed the way I felt about Leo forever.

Chapter Eight

Albert

I am not entirely sure what led us to the decision to buy another dog. Given the first 12 months with Leo had been such a challenge, I don't know how we could think having another dog would make the situation any easier. We told ourselves that it would be good for Leo to have another dog to show him what to do and become more 'dog like', plus he would have company when we were at work.

So, in July 2009 we brought home Albert, a Pug, Boston Terrier cross. 9 weeks old and 9 inches long. When we went to get him, he was asleep in a shoe. He was without a doubt the ugliest little thing I had ever seen and I knew I just had to have him. I vowed that this time would be different. We had made so many mistakes with Leo and I was determined to be a more responsible dog owner. It was a different drive home because we knew what was ahead of us. He was so small, I had no doubt he would be on my lap every single night. He was a much more nervous chap and visibly shook at loud noises and his movements hadn't properly formed yet so he resembled a really poorly edited animation as he walked around.

Bringing him into our home was very different from Leo's arrival. For a start, everyone knew what we were doing and the kids were all eagerly waiting to meet him. It went without saying that Leo would be excited. He lived in a constant state of excitement. What we were not prepared for was the insanity that became our lives for the next 3 months.

I wanted to call him Gizmo – he really did look like a gremlin, but I was outvoted. And so, Albert he was. A particular memory that has stuck with me was feeding him that evening. We put some food down in a saucer and he climbed in and laid on top of it – spread out as if protecting it. This was, we were to discover, just one of his many quirks. We lost him a number of times in the first few days – any tiny gap he would climb into and disappear. He would get shut into bedrooms and it became a part of the daily routine to 'find Albert'. He was not a happy chap. He was serious and fairly grumpy. He just wanted to eat, sleep and live life on his terms. Leo had other ideas. Never in my wildest dreams did I imagine how difficult it would be to bring a new puppy into a house where Leo lived. Don't get me wrong – they didn't fight. Quite the opposite. Leo just simply would not leave Albert alone for a second. He was constantly licking him and jumping around him. Tiny Albert soon realised though that he could fit under Leo's belly and run away.

Luckily Albert was crate trained so was happy to lay in there and quite possibly relieved to be free of his crazy new brother. Leo would just lay beside the cage, whimpering at us to let him out. The second that Albert made any noise, Leo was up, trying to get our attention. He absolutely adored him.

They could not be left alone together for a moment. Leaving the house was even more of a mission as we had to separate them and Leo was far from happy about it. On more than one occasion, I questioned our decision to get another dog. It was so stressful. I imagined them playing happily together and sleeping in the same bed and being the best of friends. But Albert was not a particularly friendly dog and was far from overjoyed about the amount of relentless attention he was getting from Leo. He just wanted to be left alone in peace. Leo just wanted to lick him, all day long. So, wherever Albert went, Leo went. If Albert was having a cuddle on my lap, Leo was jumping up and squashing us to get a cuddle also.

Walking Albert for the first few times was unexpectedly difficult because he simply refused to move. We would put his lead on, step outside and he would just lay down on the concrete and not budge. This was new. What was this all about? No amount of encouragement, cajoling or calling would shift him. So, we carried him to the park, whilst

Leo jumped all the way there, trying to get to him. Fortunately, this did not last very long and soon Albert was happy to go for a walk. So was Leo. He was so happy that he would run round and round Albert, tangling up the leads, jumping, licking and quite honestly, winding me up. It was so stressful. I had no idea that another dog would behave so differently. He was the polar opposite of Leo in almost every way. He had no interest in anything other than a tennis ball which we had to withdraw from our walks because he became so obsessed with it. A couple of times other dogs have grabbed it and it hasn't ended well. He did not understand play and although most dogs got the message pretty quickly and either laid down in front of him, or took off for the hills, if any persistent breeds wanted to play he would snap at them. It was exacerbated by the fact the Leo *loved* to play and would be bounding about with all the dogs and Albert would look on, unsure as to whether he needed to step in and rescue him.

He didn't reserve this attitude just for other dogs, he wasn't a fan of humans either, particularly men. One time, we had almost finished our walk on the beach and he started to run in the opposite direction, towards an elderly gentleman who was several steps behind us. He stopped in front of him and just started barking relentlessly. The poor man didn't even have a dog with him! I called him back and he got half way before he ran back again and again, non-stop barking. To this day I have no idea why. Luckily the man laughed it off as I got him on his lead so he could pass by us. His general reaction to anyone approaching me is to bark at them but this was definitely odd, even for him. Of course, there was the odd exception where he would run off up to someone, sit at their feet and give them the 'puppy eyes,' which never failed to get him attention. He really was just the strangest little chap.

If Leo had a ball, Albert would take it and Leo would look at me as if to say, 'that's mine,' but he never challenged him. And so little Albert soon became the boss. He got whatever he wanted because Leo was more than happy to give it to him. Of course, now, they are a happy(ish) pair of friends. Leo still adores him and Albert is still very much in charge. I think they have been good for each other and Albert has had his own lessons to teach us. He has come with his own set of challenges, particularly to do with his health which has given us many nights of worry and upset. He is terrified of the vet, to the point where he once got so upset his eyeball ruptured and he almost lost it. Like anything you want to avoid, the annual check-ups always seem to come around too quickly. As the vets struggle to get near him, Michael has to cover him with a blanket, grip him tightly under his arm whilst he gets his jabs and screams like a Banshee. He doesn't like to get up early, instead he stays under a cover in his bed until there is something worth getting up for. He loves a squeaky toy and howls in delight for a few short minutes before he has ripped it apart and returned back to bed, leaving Leo the remnants. Despite his quirky ways, he has enriched our lives as I imagine all dogs do to their owners.

Chapter Nine

My Dog is an A**e

Over the course of the last decade there have been countless wonderful moments that we have shared with Leo. There have also been some toe-curling, mortifying moments when you want the ground to swallow you up. Here are a couple of the latter. I can laugh about it now and we have spoken about them many times, but when I was in the middle of these situations, I was embarrassed beyond belief and clueless as to what to do.

Please do not judge me.

Sunday Sunbathers

Picture the scene. A glorious Sunday morning. Not a cloud in the sky. As it is peak holiday season we have come to the beach early before it gets too busy. There are a handful of fellow dog walkers in the distance but that is all. I scan my immediate area and it appears safe from potential disasters. So Leo, Albert and I began a nice slow walk along the grassy path, somewhere between the sea and the promenade. As there was no one near us I am feeling relaxed and content, just soaking up the atmosphere and enjoying the sunshine. Due to their breed, they can struggle with their breathing in the heat, but they were trotting alongside me beautifully and in that very moment any onlooker would have thought, 'She's got her sh*t together,' as we walked in unison.

In the blink of an eye and for reasons known only to Leo, he suddenly shoots off to the left of us, towards the sea, with an unusual urgency. I knew immediately in my gut that he was not coming back, but I called after him anyway. I yelled, I screamed and it just seem to propel him further forward. I looked at Albert and then we both started to run.

Just for the record, I don't run.

Leo hasn't looked back once. He slowed down slightly as he climbed the small mound of pebbles that preceded the sea. Once over it, he vanished from sight.

It was then that I heard the screams.
As we reached the pebbles, gasping for air, Albert and I scoured the scene before us. Then we spotted him. A couple were laying out on the sand, sunbathing and Leo had made a beeline for them. He was jumping all over the woman as she waved her arms around and tried to fight him off. He then ran around to the man and began to lick the top of his bald head. The woman was screaming, which I am sure Leo took as, 'I love it, please continue.'

My arrival only added to the excitement as I tried to apologise and take control of the situation.

Instead, I found myself running in circles around the couple, whilst Leo was out in front having the time of his life. After what seemed an age, I managed to grab hold of him and get the lead on. He was panting, I was panting, and the woman was verging on hyperventilating. I was also absolutely raging. I could feel the couples' eyes on me, no doubt judging me for my inability to control this crazy fur ball of a dog. No one spoke. I couldn't bring myself to look at them. Holding tight onto his lead we turned back for home. Albert was sitting, bolt upright on the pebbles. His little face was full of disappointment and I am sure, if he could, he would have shook his head at me. It was a silent walk home.

Break for Freedom
Our busy lives left little time for a weekly food shop so we had our groceries delivered every Saturday morning. We had a routine and there was much toing and froing as we all pitched in to get the crates unpacked. Leo was his usual crazy self, running up and down the hall, following us and jumping up, trying to grab the shopping out of our hands. We had attempted to train him to help us with the shopping by giving him some of the non-breakable, non-edible items like the kitchen roll, but he would just run off with it and we would end up chasing him all over the house.

Whilst I am not apportioning blame, this particular Saturday we did have an unusually chatty delivery driver and I soon got caught up in a conversation with him at the front door. I wasn't paying attention to what else was going on as I could hear the children were busy putting the shopping away. Up until then, I had never credited Leo with any sort of intelligence, in fact quite the opposite, I thought he was stupid. I did not suspect for a minute that he would recognise an opportunity even though it was right in front of him. But that is exactly what he did and ever so quickly and ever so quietly, he jumped over the crate of shopping that was blocking the door and was off on an adventure to the park down the road. I caught sight of him out of the corner of my eye. What followed next was nothing short of total pandemonium.

As we piled out of the door, my immediate thought was that he was going to get run over. We lived on a busy road right next to a roundabout. There was a good chance that this was not going to end well.

I spotted Leo running across the road in front of me. He was running faster than he ever had in his entire life. We were all calling his name, which was an absolute waste of time, but we did it anyway. As I got a bit closer, he turned to look at me, his face full of joy, clearly enjoying himself. I reached out to grab his collar and he darted off to the left and back into the road. There was a car approaching.

"STOP THAT CAR!!" I screamed to the kids. Thankfully, the driver obliged. More cars were coming as Leo ran off in the opposite direction, jumping on and off the path. I cannot imagine what a sight we were, chasing this puppy, shouting directions and instructions to each other. We eased closer and closer to him and eventually he was on the roundabout and he was surrounded. We had all taken a corner and were standing in the middle of the road, ready to pounce. Cars were waiting in all directions.

"NOW!!" I shouted and we all ran onto the roundabout and Leo stopped still for a second and then continued to run round in circles. The children grabbed hold of him to keep him still long enough for me to pick him up. We thanked the drivers and made a hasty retreat home. I was so embarrassed. The delivery driver was still waiting by the front door, chuckling to himself. He had clearly enjoyed the show. He hadn't even unpacked the shopping.

Jumpers for Goal Posts

The local park was just a couple of minutes from our home and was the most favoured place for walks. We were able to let him off the lead and run off some of that energy. A few laps around the perimeter was usually enough to calm him down for a while and required minimal effort on our part. We were careful to choose the best time to avoid any stressful situations. So not early, *early* morning, when all the proper dog owners were about. The ones who made everything about owning a dog look a complete doddle. Before Leo, I would see these groups of people and thought nothing of it. I paid them no mind as their dogs trotted by obediently whilst the owners casually chatted to one another. Or sitting outside a café, enjoying a latte whilst the dog slept under the table.

On this particular day, the park was not its usual quiet haven. It was full of children. Running, screaming, shouting children. We looked at each other in confusion. It was the school holidays. We had forgotten. Michael reassured me that it would be fine. Filled with apprehension, we entered the park. We began our walk, staying very close to the edge. Leo was off the lead and loving it. We didn't take our eyes off him for a second. The tension was palpable. Why couldn't the kids go and play somewhere else? What if he ran up to a child? What if a child ran up to him? What would he do? Jump, definitely. He might knock them over if they were little. I continued thinking of every bad scenario as we strolled round in silence.

In the far corner there was a football match underway. A group of boys were looking very serious and shouting to one another. As is the tradition, the goal posts were marked out with their clothing. Four coats were thrown onto the grass as they fought against each other for winning goal. I immediately wanted to head off in another direction to avoid them completely. Leo had other ideas.

He ran over to one of the coats laying on the ground. The boys were too engrossed in their game to notice. I knew if I did anything Leo would end up in the middle of the make shift pitch and cause complete chaos. We stood and watched. After much sniffing of the coat Leo made a decision. It wasn't a good decision and Michael and I watched with mouths open wide as he cocked his leg and peed all over it. It wasn't just a sprinkle. It was substantial. We exchanged glances. We called him and to my utter astonishment he came bounding over. We quickly attached his lead and left via the nearest gate. To this day I have no idea if anyone else witnessed this. I am truly sorry to the boy who had to go home and explain to his Mum that his coat was covered in wee.

Chapter Ten

The Energetic Bond

It may seem somewhat far-fetched, but having a dog
has taught me so much, not just about them, but also
about myself. I began to realise that the way that I
acted had a direct effect on the dogs' behaviour.
There was so much more to it than that, though.
I started to see myself through different eyes. If I
had such a profound effect on an animal, what
effect was I having on those around me? My dogs
were telling me in their own way to relax and calm
down.

  If I was calm, they would be calm. They
were trying to protect me when it should have been
the other way around. Albert was never relaxed,
constantly primed to jump to my defence. This
realisation made me feel terribly guilty. I was
finally starting to understand.

  On days when I was ill, or feeling down,
Leo would come and lay his head on my lap.
Somehow, he knew. He loved me unconditionally.
For the first time in my life, I felt real, tangible love

for an animal. This was a connection unlike any other that I had ever experienced.

Seeing the dogs run around on the beach and into the sea, genuinely lifted my spirits. Years on, I now realise that this was the first step on a long journey of self-discovery and awareness to find a more peaceful and fulfilling life.

All of this, from a PUG!

To be able to move on from the scary thoughts of the past and live a different reality is something I am truly grateful for. To have the bond with an animal that keeps you in the here and now, makes you forget all the trivial nonsense of everyday life and makes you focus on what is truly important. Seeing the dogs happy and safe is the best feeling in the world and whilst I know that I have given them a happy and fulfilled life, the gift that they have given me is absolutely priceless. I do not see a future that does not include dogs. Life would seem far too empty and boring. I cannot imagine coming home and there is no wagging tail there to greet me, or having no bundle of fur curled up on my lap every evening.

Years on, I hardly recognise myself. Let's be clear, I am not a 'Dog Whisperer', but we have a fairly comfortable routine and both dogs pretty much do what they are told. Unless it involves visitors, the doorbell, another dog, food, a football, etc.

I said earlier that I cannot imagine my life without a dog. Being able to take care of them and share the joy that they bring seems somewhat selfish for what I would get in return. A daily reminder to focus on what is important and find joy in all of the little things that life has to offer.

Chapter Eleven

And Baby makes Three

No, we didn't get another dog. We got a
Granddaughter.

There were countless things I was not
prepared for when it came to being a Grandmother
(but that's a whole other blog), but what I
absolutely was not expecting, was to revert back to
my childhood and feel the fear around dogs once
again. It was different this time as it was not about
me. I didn't realise it was happening straight away.
Not until the first time we had the baby overnight
and my irrational fear went into overdrive. I was so
tense and stressed and could not take my eyes off
Leo, even though the baby was tucked up in a pram,
out of harms reach.

As you can appreciate, we had done our
utmost to keep Leo away from small children, and
he had certainly never encountered a baby before. I
can honestly say he had *never* been so excited. The
look on his face when she cried was just priceless
and he sat guard by her pram or by the bedroom

door. He would come and tell us when she was awake and would jump around when we got her up. He just wanted to sniff (at) her, which terrified me, even though I knew with all my heart that he would not hurt her, I couldn't help but feel afraid.

As she began to move, my fear increased because now she could get to him! I knew deep down that it was all in my head, but it was a feeling that I knew so well that it just felt like home. I was torn between wanting her to grow up being surrounded by dogs and harbouring no fear, and wanting to protect her and keeping the dogs completely away from her.

I do just want to add here that I now realise that it was because of me that Leo reacted the way that he did around the baby. My stress levels and energy were almost tangible, especially in the early days when the baby was so small. Leo was never at fault and has only ever shown her love and affection.

Thankfully, my husband stepped in once again. Being a much more rational human being, his patience, calm and complete disregard for my craziness, has resulted in Leo and my Granddaughter becoming the best of friends. She loves to walk him on the lead, (at the end of his walk when he's worn out) and he loves to just follow her everywhere she goes. He does still get overexcited now and then, but she is more than capable and confident of telling him off! It is wonderful to watch them on the beach together.

Now she is now three and he still worships her. He just wants to lick her face constantly and she wants to pull on his curly tail. I pray that we have him long enough that they can become friends when she is a bit older and she will remember him.

I am so grateful my granddaughter can see that these are amazing animals and nothing to be afraid of. To have this instilled in her from an early age, I am hopeful that this will become a way of life for her and she will learn to appreciate the wonder of the outdoors, the sea and how good it feels to be outside with your dog.

Chapter Twelve

The World's Best Antidepressant

Some years ago, I suffered from chronic depression, resulting, at its worst, in agoraphobia which kept me a prisoner in my own home. The advice was always the same. Apart from the medication, I needed to push myself and go outside. Exercise and fresh air were my prescription. It sounds so simple and obvious. To me, back then, it sounded like hell.

Whilst I am happy to report that I no longer suffer with this debilitating illness, it has never completely gone away. There is a constant greyish-black cloud hanging over me but I am now much better equipped to stop it in its tracks.

Having the dogs has really helped me and given me a reason to go out every day, even if every fibre of my being is screaming not to. Somehow, knowing that their needs were being met was enough of a reason to get up. Clearly taking care of my own needs did not rate as highly.

I know I have already said this, but it has been paramount to my mental health. Walking on the beach with my 'boys' in the sunshine is one of my most favourite things to do and it never fails to make me smile. It lifts my spirits and stops me from overthinking, at least for the hour that we are out. I focus totally on them and leave all my worries and insecurities behind. Their needs are simple and their love is unconditional. To come from a day at work to be greeted by a happy face and crazy, wagging tail is something I never tire of. They do not judge, they just love and want to be loved.

I know without a doubt, when I used to have a black cloud kind of day, I would wallow in self-pity and stay in bed which will only compound the way I felt. Having these dogs has helped me in ways I could never have imagined. Just knowing that the dogs were relying on me gave me enough strength to get up and go out with them.

I often hear people saying that a leopard cannot change its spots – well I am living proof that they can! My entire outlook on life has changed as a result of having these dogs and I am truly grateful that I learned this lesson and I wish that I could bottle up that feeling and share it with the world. I have gone from being a quite selfish and judgemental human being to someone who finds happiness in the small and simple things in life. Seeing Leo's face first thing in the morning as he waits outside my bedroom door is a wonderful start to the day. He rolls over for a belly-rub and I can never say no.

To be able to tell this story is, in itself a gift. It has given me a purpose and an opportunity to support other rescue pugs. It has helped me connect with others that I would not have otherwise have known and has given me the push that I have needed to write my very first book.

To be able to move on from the scary thoughts of the past and live a different reality is something I am truly grateful for. To have the bond with an animal that keeps you in the here and now, makes you forget all the trivial nonsense of everyday life and makes you focus on what is truly important.

Chapter Thirteen

The Club

Growing up with older parents has equipped me with a number of so-called 'old fashioned' outlooks. One of these being my attitude towards fashion and trends. Practicality would win every time. I have always bought things for their function, not for their popularity. At least, I used to in the days before Leo. I have always shied away from trends, hearing my Mother's voice in my ear telling me what a waste of money it was. Birthday cards would simply say 'Happy Birthday', after all that was the point of them. T-shirts were plain, socks were value multipacks and everything else in my home was practical beyond belief. I am only now realising how sad this made me.

Fast forward a few years and I am now the proud owner of Pug cushions, (Pug) t shirts, (Pug) mugs, (Pug) books, cards, the list goes on. Even my make-up bag and mirror has Pugs on it. These items are not always purchased to support a charity or Pug rescue organisation. They are cleverly marketed to people like me that have an overwhelming love for their squishy pet and are making millions out of us. Even knowing this does not stop me from buying the stuff.

I am now a member of a number of Pug groups on Facebook and follow pug owners on Instagram. Even the notebook that I used to write this very story has a pug on the front of it. I can't really explain it but there is something that touches me about all of this stuff that I feel that I need it in my life. It's kind of like belonging to an exclusive sort of club. As a bona fide pug owner, I am somehow allowed to own all this stuff and people's reactions are always the same – they love it just as much as I do. It is almost like a badge of honour, which I wear with pride.

Chapter Fourteen

Poorly Pup

Unlike Albert, Leo has been mostly healthy. Yes, he was overweight, his teeth were rotten and his breath was rancid, but otherwise he was as healthy as the proverbial horse. However, one evening, I thought he was going to die right in front of me.

It was the middle of summer and we had taken our touring caravan to the coast for the weekend. It had been a very hot day and Leo had not been himself. The heat was almost as intense that evening as it had been all through the day. He was fidgety and restless, jumping onto the chair then jumping off it. No matter where he sat, he didn't seem to be able to settle. He did struggle with the heat, but there was just something about his erratic behaviour that told me he wasn't quite right. I signalled to Michael who swiftly took him outside. Seconds later Leo collapsed to the floor. He lost control of his bowels and was completely 'out of it'. Albert could sense there was something wrong and was trying to get to him as we sat together, looking through the window. Michael was gently stroking him and talking to him. The tears were pouring down my face. I was convinced he was never going to get back up. Albert's cries were just making me worse. My sobs were getting louder. He wasn't moving. Michael kept looking up at me. I knew exactly what he was thinking. I have no idea how long we sat there. All I could think was please, get up. PLEASE GET UP. It could have only been a couple of minutes or it could have been an hour. It felt like a lifetime. I was imagining having to tell the kids the worst news. How on earth would I tell Michaela? She would be heartbroken. We all would be. It was too unbearable to contemplate. I felt completely helpless. All we could do was sit, wait and pray.

And then he lifted his head. He looked up at Michael as if to say 'what the hell am I doing here?' I wanted to run out, screaming and pick him up, but I knew that wasn't what he needed. Michael continued to stroke him and talk to him as his wobbly legs failed to let him stand, so he laid, panting heavily. He had had a seizure, probably due to the heat. They had both had seizures before but nothing on this scale. Albert knocked himself out on the beach one time after he ran into a wooden post at full speed. He was out cold but was up within a couple of minutes and wanting to chase his ball. This was most definitely not like that. Eventually, Leo was strong enough to get up and was soon laying on my bed, as if nothing had happened. I stayed up with him all night, terrified that it may happen again. Thankfully, the next day he was back to his normal, mischievous self, albeit a little bit slower. Thankfully, this was an isolated incident and we have taken extra care to ensure he is cool and comfortable on those really hot summer days.

Chapter Fifteen

Why Do They Do That?

Even after all this time I am still baffled at some of the things these dogs get up to.

For example, on a hot day, we will open up the patio doors into the garden. Leo will always shoot straight outside, run around to the back door and sit there until I let him back in. Why doesn't he come back in through the patio door?

Why, when he is hungry, why does Leo pick up his food bowl and throw it outside? The dog food is kept in the kitchen? He will sit by the back door, looking at it and it is only when I go looking for him that I realise what he is doing.

When I have treats they come and sit by my feet, giving me their most angelic smiles. They take one each and whilst Leo makes off with his at lightning speed, Albert refuses his and lets it fall on the floor. He then follows Leo, watching him chew, cough and splutter his way through his treat. They exchange eye contact and just like that, Leo drops it. Albert grabs it and Leo goes over to Albert's treat and starts chewing that. A couple of minutes later, when Albert has finished, he once again stares at Leo and ever so compliantly, Leo surrenders it and Albert takes it off him and eats it, right in front of him. Leo never complains.

Standing at the back door together and only one will go out. The other refuses and just walks away. I sit down, then one wants to come back in. the other is still not interested so I sit down again and only then will they go to the door to be let out!

Why do they know where to lay so they are right in front of the door of the room that you want to go in?

What is it about a closed door? They are irresistible to Leo. If we are in the kitchen and I close the door, he will sit in front of it until I open it. He walks through and looks at me and then comes back in. He then sits in front of the door again. It doesn't matter where we are, what door, or staircase, he has to go through it to come back in again. When I come home and open the back door, he will step out of the door and sit outside. Then I shut the door and he will then scratch at the door to come in. It drives me nuts!

Why does he follow me EVERYWHERE? At first I thought it was a puppy thing but it is definitely a Leo thing. I am never out of his sight. Albert can hardly be bothered to get up and see me when I come home from work, let alone follow me around. I have lost count of the number of times I have tripped over him because I've walked into a room then out again and he has plonked himself in the middle of the doorway, no doubt trying to work out if I'm staying in this space or not.

Why will they eat full fat yogurt but not the diet variety?? I have tested this out countless times and regardless of brand or flavour, if it has 'diet' on it, they refuse to touch it.

Chapter Sixteen

The Woman on the Beach

I saw someone on the beach this morning and the sight of her instantly took me back to my childhood. The knot in my stomach, the instinctive clenching of my fists and the waves of nausea came flooding back to me.

It was early, around 07:30 and the dogs and I were nearing the end of our walk. The beach was unusually quiet and as we approached the promenade, heading for home, a woman appeared a few metres behind us. There was something about her body language that made me feel drawn to her. It felt familiar. She was too far away for me to talk to so ignoring the feeling in my gut, I carried on.

The last part of our walk is always a long and drawn out affair. As soon as we reach a certain point – the final set of beach steps - their exuberance and energetic charging about is replaced by what can only be described as pathetic shuffling along at a snails' pace. In addition, every single blade of grass between that point and home has to be sniffed within an inch of its life. They also like to feign interest in some grain of sand which just happens to be in the opposite direction to which we are going. This results in a lot of stopping and waiting around. I have learned over the years that the more I complain about this, the longer it will take, particularly if I am working against the clock and have to be somewhere.

As Leo trotted off in the opposite direction, to find his latest treasure, I noticed that the woman stopped in her tracks. Despite the distance between us I could sense her panic. Fortunately, on this occasion, Leo became distracted by a pile of rabbit poo so he stopped for further examination. I called him back as I quickly glanced up at the woman who hadn't moved from the spot. I encouraged him back and we continued on our slow walk home.

I was keen to get going as I could feel the agitation rising within me, although I had no idea why. I just felt like I wanted to get off the beach as soon as possible so that nothing 'bad' could happen.

Cue Leo.

He took off. Running towards the woman. She had frozen. I called him, (just for the hell of it). He kept running. Albert then decided to compound the situation by barking. Being such a little thing, his bark is more amusing than aggressive, but nonetheless, I could see it had made the woman jump. And then I realised. She was afraid. She took a couple of hesitant steps forward and once again stopped. She was trying to work out if it was safe for her to continue or if Leo was going to approach her. His size was irrelevant. Fear is rarely rational. There must have been something in my voice as I called out to Leo because he turned straight round and ran back to me. I put his lead on, hoping this would reassure her. We looked at each other for what seemed the longest time, then she turned around and hurried away, no doubt embarrassed that I had witnessed that.

My heart went out to her. I knew just how she was feeling. I wanted to run after her, to reassure her that the dogs were not scary and wouldn't hurt her. I knew that this encounter had the potential to ruin her day and she may dwell on it, making the next walk that she attempted even more of a challenge. As the dogs watched me, no doubt wondering what on earth I was doing, I felt so very sad. Their eager little faces were looking up at me and in that moment I felt an overwhelming surge of gratitude. To think that I could have missed out on having them in my life was almost too much to bear. I felt so fortunate to have learned to love these animals and allow them to enrich my life.

I hope that one day the woman on the beach gets to be as lucky as me.

Chapter Seventeen

Who Will Look After My (Fur) Babies?

I have previously touched on our decision to stick to dog-friendly UK holidays. The idea of leaving them behind was simply not an option although we have never been a family that has been hugely interested in travel. So we explored Suffolk's Heritage Coast in our touring caravan (and found our current home). It is fair to say that we all had a great time. Plenty of walks, unlimited amounts of chicken and unlimited cuddles. Our activities were somewhat restricted – we couldn't go out for meals and our days out had to be dog friendly, but I wouldn't have had it any other way.

We did manage the odd night away, now and again, when the kids were at home, but even then I demanded constant updates and photos to ensure that they were ok.

And then my Kayla announced she was getting married. In CYPRUS.

Now, I am not going to say that this was the *first* thing that came into my head but it was definitely up there. What on earth were we going to do with the dogs for two whole weeks?? How was I ever going to find any kind of doggy day care that would understand how I felt about them? And secondly, they were so badly behaved, they wouldn't fit into a 'normal' routine. They were used to freedom, comforts and constant love and attention. Who on earth was going to provide all of that plus peace of mind and reassurance that they were being looked after?

I made some tentative enquiries through fellow dog owners, but they mostly had family that looked after their pooches. My family was all going to be in Cyprus with us!

I searched social media and the internet. Of the handful of places that seemed like they might be able to cater to the dogs' needs, all of them were full. As the date grew closer, the task began to feel overwhelming.

I didn't understand it. I mean, we had found babysitters for the kids on numerous occasions and I had never given it a second thought! There was definitely an element of embarrassment at my inability to have gained 'control' of my dogs. I didn't want a so called 'expert' to judge me or them.

Michael suggested we go and visit a kennels. We were desperate. I really did not want to go, but I also knew we were running out of options and time. The short drive to the kennels was silent. "Give it a chance," Michael said. I didn't reply. As we pulled in, I could hear the dogs barking. I had knots in my stomach. 'There is no way they are staying here,' I thought to myself. We got out and we were greeted by one of the owners. I explained the situation. 'They have never been left,' I said. The man looked at me with surprise. What, *NEVER*? I tried to make him understand their unique requirements, in particular, Albert's dislike of everyone and everything. Talking over me, he said dogs just want to be dogs, to run free together. It's the owners that have the issues not them.

Hmmmmm.

Whilst this might be true, it really wasn't what I wanted to hear. I said very little else as I was raging inside. We were given a quick tour of the kennels and as the dogs jumped up to see us, I just wanted to burst into tears. We left soon after. Kennels were not discussed again.

I want to add a caveat here. I know many dog owners whose dogs are very happy and well looked after in kennels, particularly those who have succeeded with a routine, crate training and socialisation etc. As I had failed in all of the above areas, I knew that this particular environment was not suitable for my dogs. I realised that I needed someone to take care of them in their own home.

I approached another couple of people, but their responses were less than enthusiastic. Why did nobody understand? Surely, I was not the only dog owner who had this problem? Surely there were other hopeless dog owners out there that spoiled their dogs and gave into their every whim?

I was losing hope, fast.

And then, I found her. I can't even remember how. She just appeared one day, on my social media feed, and I just knew she was the one. Another Angel.

'*Hatty's Hounds offers a bespoke luxury un-kennelled accommodation in our country home. Your dogs will be able to enjoy full use of our home where they can use our range of soft, luxury beds doggy sofas, blankets, plush toys and teddies. They will also have full use of our safe, secure, pretty meadows and gardens, where they can both relax and exercise at their leisure. Your dogs will be very loved and you can be assured of their safety, happiness and well-being whilst in our care.*'

I mean, *I* wanted to go for a holiday there! We arranged to visit and despite painting the worst possible picture of their behaviour, I was still worried that she would be horrified, refuse to take them and send me packing with a flea in my ear about dog training, boundaries, manners etc. etc. I was prepared for most scenarios, but not what actually happened when we arrived.

There was no jumping, no barking, no pooing, no craziness and no sign of any of the behaviours that I had experienced in the last decade. They trotted around politely, as if that was what they did every bloody day and even when, EVEN WHEN, they encountered another dog and my heart was in my chest, they just sniffed at one another. Albert took himself off to one of the many luxurious dog beds and Leo went outside to explore. I was speechless.

I mean WHAT THE ACTUAL HECK.......???

For a split second I thought it was as if they knew how important this was and conspired to be on their best behaviour, just so I could go on holiday and see my daughter get married. Then I realised, Louise, they are *dogs*. I didn't dwell on it, I just got us all out of there as quickly as possible before they reverted to their true feral selves.

Fast forward to October 2018 and I think it is fair to say that we all had an amazing holiday. Whilst I was crying my eyes out at Michaela's wedding, Leo and Albert were having the absolute time of their lives. They visited wonderful places along with the rest of Hatty's pack. They had fresh meat, fish and vegetables every day plus juicy bones as an afternoon treat. They were loved unconditionally. I had complete peace of mind as Hattie sent me pictures and updates every day. There was also an unexpected bonus on their return. I was so excited to see them. We had never been apart for so long. I couldn't wait for them to come charging in and run around my ankles, sniffing and snorting. I opened the door and they strolled in, barely giving me the time of day. I mean, I was glad that they had had a nice time, but, you know, they could have at least acted like they missed me! They were completely different dogs. There was not jumping or barking. They were so calm.

For the next few weeks, they was no madness when I arrived home, there was very little barking, jumping or misbehaving of any kind. It served as a further reminder to me that it was my energy and behaviour around these precious dogs of mine that had created so many of the situations I have shared.

They have been back for another holiday and exactly the same thing happened. Hatty truly has a presence around these animals that I have never witnessed before and I am so grateful to have found her.

Chapter Eighteen

Netflix & 'Chill'

In the days before Leo, Michaela would often describe cosy, peaceful evenings at home, with our well-behaved pug, who would curl up in his bed or on the sofa and sleep soundly until morning, whilst we all sat around the fire and sung Kumbaya.

I can count on one hand the number of times this has happened (not the singing).

I arrive home about 5:30 pm. I work just minutes away and have been home at lunch time so the dogs are not alone for long. I open the back door and stand back. Leo comes charging out in a scene that could be mistaken for me returning from a five-year duty of Iraq. There is snorting, jumping, and ferocious tail wagging and running round and round my feet in circles. I can't quite navigate around him so I have to wait until he has finished.

I step in the kitchen and Albert strolls in to see what all the fuss is about. "Oh, it's you," his look of disappointment is evident as he walks back to his bed. Leo follows me around as I get on with chores and gets under my feet whilst I cook dinner.

They both sit at my feet whilst I eat. I choose to believe it is a gesture of love, but deep down I know that they are just there in the hope that I drop my dinner on the floor.

It is soon time to sit down. The dogs have been waiting in the hall for me, watching my every move. I get a fresh fluffy blanket and position myself on the sofa. Within seconds Albert is on my lap and Leo is by my side, licking my arm. Clicking on the remote, I select the movie I have been wanting to watch for a while. Leo's gentle snoring is Albert's cue to climb under the blanket. He settles down and lets out a big sigh. Perfect. We are all relaxed. Feeling content with my lot, I put my feet up and press play. The titles start to roll.

Meanwhile, in a remote village on the North Norfolk border, someone, (probably a man), sneezes, coughs or farts. Within a nano-second this noise has reached my dogs' sensitive ear drums and they are both up. All signs of restful, peaceful slumber completely obliterated. Replaced with barking jumping, running from one room to another to find the source of the noise.

I get up. They are at the back door. I open it and they fly out to investigate the garden for signs of the intruder. They bark at the gate, I'm guessing they are interrogating it and this continues until I can no longer put up with it and I bring them inside.

I return to the sofa and we get settled. Albert is under the blanket and Leo is snoring his head off. I click the remote and lay back in the chair. In 30 minutes, I have only managed to watch the titles.

My next door neighbour pulls onto his drive. Leo is up. Albert is up. Cue barking, jumping and running in circles. Five minutes later we are in the back garden, examining the gate for clues. It starts to rain. We traipse back in. Leo looks at his empty food bowl and then at me. Albert sniffs at the water bowl and looks at me – it needs refreshing. So, like a good and patient dog owner, I oblige. Once fed and watered, I open the back door and tell them to go toilet because I want to sit down. They both look away.

"Ok, but I'm not getting up for at least an hour so you will just have to wait," I march, somewhat defiantly, back to my sofa. Albert has beaten me to it and is already in my spot, on top of my blanket. After some gentle persuasion, he reluctantly lets me back in my seat. I wait a few minutes before reaching for the remote, just to be sure they are finally settled. I have to hit rewind as I have completely forgotten what I was watching. Ten minutes in and all is calm. I can feel myself starting to relax.

Then, Albert lets out a huge fart.

"Oh my God, Albert, that STINKS!" I yell as I jump up from my seat to escape the foul stench. He looks unimpressed as the blankets gets pulled off him. Leo doesn't look too pleased about being disturbed either. I hear myself *apologising* and once again, for the fourth time that evening, I take my seat on the sofa. It is now nine o'clock.

Leo jumps off the sofa and walks into the kitchen. I pretend I haven't notice, but I turn down the TV and listen intently to work out what he is up to. Silence. The kind of silence when a two year old is unravelling the toilet roll or has found your make up bag.

"He is fine," I tell myself. A couple more minutes go by. I am sitting up, waiting. Not sure what for. I can't hear him eating or drinking or doing anything. With a sigh I pull off the blanket and go into the kitchen. He is laying on the floor, waiting for me. We have a conversation, at least, I ask him what he is doing. He rolls onto his back for a belly rub. I instantly obey. I tell him he's my baby whilst I am rubbing his huge tummy. Hair is flying everywhere.

I get up and return to the sofa. I am sure Albert is laughing at me. We don't make eye contact. There is no sign of Leo. This dog follows me everywhere, even to the loo, and he has decided to stay in the kitchen. I call him, trying to sound casual. It doesn't work.

"I am not getting up again," I say, boldly. I could be mistaken, but I am sure I heard a little snigger.
"FINE! Stay there then!"

Feeling somewhat dramatic, I turn up the TV, but I am not really watching it. All the time I am listening to the deafening silence coming from the kitchen.

"Ok, you win!" I say 5 minutes later as I fling off the blanket. Albert groans and I reply "Tell me about it," and I storm off back into the kitchen.

Leo is sitting by the back door, with his special puppy eyes. He wants to go toilet. I instantly feel bad and once again, I am apologising. I let him out. He is gone for ages and refuses to come back in. He sits outside the back door then once I open it he looks the other way. This goes on for some time until finally he relents and ambles in at a snail's pace. As we head back to the sofa, Albert is sitting on the floor in the hall. "What do you want?" I ask. He runs to the back door and I let him out, whilst muttering to myself. On our final attempt to get comfy, I realise it is now ten o'clock. They have both jumped onto my blanket on the sofa before me. I admit defeat. I turn off the TV, having watched just the titles and whilst they both snore their heads off, I complain to them about their appalling behaviour. That is before I give them a kiss good night and head off to bed.

Chapter Nineteen

Book Launch Day
(Just for Fun)

11pm. Leo and Albert are laying on the sofa on the hooman's favourite, freshly washed, fluffy blanket, talking about their day. She has just gone to bed.

"She has been a nightmare today, worse than usual," Albert complains as Leo nods in agreement. "Book this, book that, book everything else. She has been banging on about it for days. It got so bad this afternoon I had to summon the killer fart just to get her to leave me in peace for 5 minutes."

"But we have had so many treats today! I've never eaten so much cheese!" Leo licks his lips in appreciation. "Apparently, we are celebrating."

"How do you know that?" Albert's ears prick up. "She has been crying most of the day."

"She's been on that fizzy drink and the posh glasses have come out of the cupboard. You know, the ones with my face on," Leo sneezes all over the blanket.

"Man, all we want is to chill out on the beach. What's all the fuss about?" Albert shakes his head and then turns to look at Leo.

"Hey," he whispers. Leo looks up. Albert raises his paw. Leo does the same. "High Five, Man, you're famous!"

Leo giggles. "Ha-ha that means I can get away with even more now. Bring it on Bro!" And with a final nod, they snuggle down, lick the blanket and drift off to sleep.

Chapter Twenty

Do I Look Like my Dog?
(Just for Fun)

I am a people watcher. I absolutely love it. I make up stories in my head about where the person is going, what their life is like and it is always extraordinary, or else, what is the point? Recently, though, I have developed a new game, called 'who owns that dog?'

Living on the coast, there is an abundance of dog owners and during the holiday season the village is packed. So when I encounter a dog for the first time, I like to scan the area and see if I can match him to his owner! Sometimes it is so obvious and it really makes me smile. I have found that Greyhounds in particular have very distinctive looking owners.

This is of course, just a bit of harmless fun and not intended to offend anyone.

There are almost always similarities. Our daughter, Kayla, is a prime example as she has a Dalmatian who is very graceful, slender and athletic which mirrors her owner perfectly.

Then I got to thinking that surely this would also apply to me and then the more I thought about it, the more it made sense. Our similarities were obvious!

- Sheds hair at an alarming rate
- Bad teeth
- Overweight
- Grey hair
- Inappropriate
- Guaranteed to embarrass you in social situations
- No concept of boundaries
- Does whatever he wants, when he wants
- Obsessed with food
- Snores
- Undeniably cute

There is no right or wrong answer but I do have to admit that the evidence is overwhelming.

Chapter Twenty One

The Wonder of Dogs

I have read countless stories about dogs and their amazing acts of courage and bravery. Saving lives, alerting their owners of danger, sniffer dogs, guide dogs, and the list goes on and on.

To date, none of these dogs (to my knowledge), have been Pugs. Stereotypical superhero dogs are mostly Labradors and of course, the German Shepherd.

However, I would like to champion the humble Pug, for all the joy and laughter they bring to their owners' lives. You could argue that all dogs do this, but there is just something about that squishy face, curly tale and, quite honestly, lack of intelligence that puts them in a class of their own. Their desire to please you and their endless affection is undeniable.

Of all of the dog owners that I have met over the years, it is those that own Pugs that appear to have formed the strongest bonds. I do believe that every dog picks its owner, so it is no surprise that these people feel such love for their animals as it was clearly what they needed in their lives and why many of them go on to have such large packs of pugs.

Leo's unconditional love has literally changed my life and therefore, the life of my family. I would say that that is pretty wondrous, wouldn't you?

Chapter Twenty Two

The Biggest Lesson of All

Living in the moment.

It sounds easy and a lot of the time it is. When you wake up after 8 hours sleep and the sun is shining, you are off to a good start. When you can enjoy that first cup of coffee without watching the clock or thinking about the commute, your mind is open and ready to receive more and more of the good stuff. Then, you come up against something. It could be a flippant remark, a disagreement, a stressful situation, or just about anything that puts you into a negative mind set. *That* is when living in the moment is a challenge.

Dogs do not dwell on the past nor do they plan for the future. They do not think about what might or might not happen if they decide to do X, Y or Z. They are always in the here and now. I, on the other hand, am a champion over thinker, re-living scenarios again and again and creating problems in my mind that do not even exist.

So when Albert had an altercation with another dog and came off worse, my brain went into over drive. It was so unexpected and Albert was entirely to blame, so I should have been able to accept that and focus on something good. Instead, I immediately decided that I was never going to feel safe again whilst walking him. I would have to re-think the time of day that we went out, to avoid as many dog walkers as possible, (even though I did that anyway). I had completely convinced myself that on every walk we would be dicing with death and it was going to be a stressful experience as I would need to be on high alert at all times. Irrational does not even come close. And so, it *was* just that. There was no way to avoid every single dog and it was inevitable that we would come face to face with some. I would eye the owner suspiciously, looking for any clues as to an imminent attack. I don't know what I was expecting? Maybe a badge? .

As crazy as this may sound, I know that I am not alone. I have met many dog owners whose dogs are no longer let off the lead after some sort of incident. They tell me that their dog is nervous and doesn't mix well. It has been 'labelled' in order to keep it safe. I, myself have said this many times in an attempt to keep Albert out of harm's way. There was one encounter in particular that I will always remember. It was a sunny Saturday afternoon at the height of the holiday season and the beach was busy. A couple and their dog were walking towards us. As soon as I was in their eye line, a frantic conversation ensued. The man moved in front and passed the lead over as the woman followed behind. I watched with fascination as the man outstretched his arms, acting almost as some kind of human shield. I was not sure if he was protecting them or us. My face must have given me away as he began to explain the reasons for his extreme action. His dog had been involved in some sort of disagreement and as a result they went to these lengths to keep him safe. I recall this with no judgement whatsoever, I just felt incredibly sad for them as that was now their reality. It was not beyond the realms of reason that I too may find myself taking such drastic measures to keep the dogs safe. I could feel their fear and I wanted to reassure them that we posed no threat. Then I realised, if the situation had been reversed, it would have served as no comfort to me to hear this. I could see their pain so clearly and I wished that they could be brave enough to try again or at least, work on it. But who was I to share my thoughts with complete strangers when I was still not learning the lessons for myself.

I realise that I am making some sweeping generalisations here and I do not pretend to have any specialist knowledge – far from it. I know that there are always extremes in life and sadly, many dogs have suffered and as a result are traumatised. I am in no way making light of this or brushing this aside. It was merely intended to highlight, once again, how my fear can create a more stressful and challenging situation for all of us when it really does not need to be that way. Despite this understanding, it remains a daily practice to stay in the present and focus on the now.

Chapter Twenty Three

COV-ID

At the time of writing this chapter, we are coming out the other side of the lockdown as shops and restaurants are beginning to re-open.

Many people struggled with the rules that governed our reality, myself included. Despite being relatively fit and healthy and able to get out of the house, the general feeling of panic at what was happening in the world, continually played on my mind.

For me, the one constant that got me through is having the dogs. Firstly they have loved having me at home 24/7 because this translated in even more attention and a ton of extra snacks. But I know, without doubt, that there would have been days when I would not have wanted to get out of bed and gone down a rabbit hole of anxiety and fear. So at the height of lockdown, when only one, 1- hour walk was allowed, I made sure that I took them out. This then gave me momentum to do other things, such as cook a proper meal for myself and change out of my pyjamas. These small things would spur me on to achieve something else and so it continued and before I knew it, I had created a routine and the days suddenly seemed a lot less scary.

I was furloughed from work so I was lucky enough to spend the whole of the summer at home with the dogs, which I will always be grateful for. I am about to return to work and the anxious feelings I felt about staying at home have been replace with concerns about *leaving* my home and interacting with customers and work colleagues.

The words that we tell ourselves are so incredibly important. Thankfully, mental health is more commonly spoken about than ever before, but you never really know what another person is going through.

'In a world where you can be anything, be kind.'

Chapter Twenty Four

Overweight vs Underweight

Pugs are notoriously chunky dogs. Our lack of discipline has not helped Leo's physique and annual check-ups in recent years have almost always included a stern word or two regarding his weight.

Albert, on the other hand has always had a slight frame and the appearance that he needed fattening up. This has resulted in a dilemma of how to feed Albert an extra meal without Leo having any.

Now, I know what you are going to say. Those of you that are seasoned dog owners, who are sensible and responsible and are the pack leaders. It is simple. Just separate them. Feed Albert on his own. Put Leo in another room, or outside. I think you know me well enough by now to know that I am made of a much weaker moral fibre and could not bring myself to do this. Leo's cries were just too much to bear and the stress that this caused me (ok, that I created) then affected Albert's enthusiasm to eat the aforementioned food that I was trying to get him to eat in the first place.

BREATHE.

Could I have gotten it any more wrong? I doubt it. So, I caved in. I let Leo into the kitchen and he too enjoyed an extra meal (albeit a smaller portion). Albert scoffed his down. I was happy. Leo was happy and God knows, my Husband was happy. Yes, Leo got fat. Was this irresponsible of me? I am sure you have already decided this. There is no doubt that I should have been stronger. I have never claimed to be perfect and nor would I ever want to be. I did what I thought was the best thing for everyone, including me.

Albert started filling out and looking much less like an abandoned puppy that had been left by the roadside. We made sure that Leo got plenty of exercise. I made peace with it.

As the years passed, the excess weight became more of an issue. A Senior dog, or, as I like to refer to them, one in his Twilight years, can suffer joint pain and this is exacerbated by excess weight and pressure on his joints.

Conversely, Albert's weight began to plummet quite dramatically. After a series of tests, he was prescribed antibiotics which helped but he just couldn't seem to regain the weight he had lost.

It is now 7 months since this infection and we have bought supplements and drops and feed him fat-filled frankfurters but there is no real improvement. His coat is dull and his energy is low. He hasn't sprinted across the beach in the longest time. The majority of his day is now spent in his bed, watching me (and no doubt disapproving). He is 11 and I must learn to come to terms with that. I often get comments from fellow dog walkers on his decline and weight loss. So, we are back to extra meals for both of them, because, to be frank, I will do whatever I can to make him comfortable for as long as I can.

Chapter Twenty Five

A Setback

Today I witnessed an unprovoked dog on dog attack which, quite honestly, shook me to my core.

I do not feel like I want to share the specific details, other than to say that one dog set upon another for no good reason. It was aggressive and extremely distressing to witness.

Unsurprisingly, it played on my mind all day. What I was not expecting though, was all of the fears I held around dogs to resurface. I was suddenly terrified at the thought of going out for a walk in case we encountered another dog – any dog that wasn't on a lead. I imagined the most awful scenarios which continued to fuel my fears. I just did not know how to stop it. So for a few days, I once again passed over the dog walking to Michael and then I began to go out with him, walking away as soon as I saw another dog. And, inevitably, I did encounter a dog. A loud, large, barking dog. I held my breath and backed away. My heart was pounding and I felt like a little girl all over again.

I know that I need to come to terms with it. I also know it will take some time. I am now taking Leo out for his walks, but I am acutely aware of any dogs in our vicinity. I am once again choosing quieter times to go out a time and keep my focus solely on Leo. If there is what I perceive to be any kind of imminent threat, we simply leave. Some days we haven't gotten very far, but as long as I keep trying, eventually I will overcome it once again.

Chapter Twenty Six

The One I didn't want to write

On Tuesday 18th August 2020, we had to say
goodbye to our beloved Albert. He had been
steadily deteriorating before our eyes and was
losing weight rapidly. I tried everything, despite
knowing what was coming. I just was not ready to
lose him.

He became more and more withdrawn, some
days not even wanting to go for a walk and the days
he did, there was no running, just a very slow walk
which we usually cut short. Food became an issue
as he was unable to swallow it without choking so I
fed him by hand, tiny pieces of food as slowly as I
could. I would cover up his tiny, bony body as it
hurt to look at it and it was soon after that Michael
made an appointment to take him to the vet.

I knew that something was wrong because
he hadn't called me on the way home to let me
know what the vet had said. He walked into the
kitchen and reached for my hand and his words all
just merged together. Cancer, kidney failure,

growths in his throat. The vet told us to 'Enjoy your last few days together'.

That night I slept on the kitchen floor next to Albert. I slept with him every night because I couldn't bear to be parted from him. We had to decide on a date. How can you even do that? But we did and it hung over us all like a huge black cloud. Every minute that passed meant less time I had with him. It was torture. We loved him as much as we could, until it felt like my heart would burst. I still could not believe that it was actually going to happen. I prayed every single night that he would go to sleep and not wake up, that he would spend his last moments with us, in his bed at home and pass peacefully. The thought of medical intervention, no matter how kind and effective, was just too painful to even process.

And then the day came. Michael had dug a hole in the corner of the garden. We took him to the beach one last time. We sat outside in the sun whilst he slept next to us. There were no words left to say. The time went too quickly and it was soon time for one last cuddle. I held his frail body close to me and told him how much I loved him before I handed him to Michael.

An hour passed as Leo and I waited for their return. As the car pulled into the drive, I left Leo inside and went to meet them. Michael brought Albert's bed out of the car. He was wrapped up in a blanket. We took him inside and removed his bandage and cleaned him up. I had his favourite blanket all washed ready for him. We took him to the garden where Michael laid him, along with his tennis ball. We sat in the garden for hours, neither of us wanting to leave him.

The next few days were as tough as I imagined they would be. As with everything that is too painful for me to deal with, I withdrew from the outside world. I found moments when I complete forgot what had happened and would go outside and look for him or wonder where he was.

Six weeks on and it is still as raw. Leo has reacted very badly. We knew that he would show grief in some way but were not prepared for his obvious outpouring of sadness. He has woken us up for a number of nights, howling. He has begun frantic chewing on his legs. I am aware that my own sadness is playing a lead role in his behaviour and I just hope in time things will get a little easier. I want to get my boy back to his happy and crazy self once again.

Chapter Twenty Seven

It Travels Down the Lead

Before Leo, this was a term I had never heard of, and even when I did, I did not really understand its concept.

But now, after losing Albert, I completely understand it.

Although I talk to Leo as if he is human, I do know, deep down, that he has no idea what I am banging on about unless I say 'chicken.' However, I had convinced myself that this form of communication was completely acceptable; after all I had witnessed countless other dog owners do exactly the same thing and they seemed to know what they were doing (compared to me, at least). I knew Leo would be sad – whatever the dog equivalent of that is, but I never thought that my own grief would affect him in such a debilitating way.

He became more and more reluctant to go out for a walk, and then once we were out, he simply did not want to come back. This gradually got worse until one day we got out of the back door and he did not budge. There was no tail wagging and panting. There was no running around my ankles and trying to grab the lead. He just stood there, looking at the ground, with his tail hanging down. I tugged on his collar, I put on my very best excited Mum voice but nothing worked. After a few minutes I told myself that once we were actually out on the beach he would be fine. So I tugged and pulled him onto the drive. Once again, he stopped. And then, he just turned back and starting pulling to go back inside. I was gobsmacked as it suddenly dawned on me what the problem was. I was also incredibly sad. So we went back inside. He took himself off to sit by Albert's favourite spot and I went off for yet another cry. He was so sad, and my own grief was just too much for him to bear. He had picked up on my emotional state and had just said 'I can't do this.' I don't blame him, I mean, I didn't want to be around me either, let alone go out and possibly encounter a human that is going to ask why I only have one dog.

Hatty has worded this beautifully and I know she is happy for me to share this with you all;

Communication through the lead:

Leads are one of the most powerful tools of connecting dog to human. Dogs are masters of reading our emotions and the lead is like a direct link between our brains & bodies and theirs.

Through a lead you're constantly communicating with your dog via speed, pattern of movement and tension (among other things) while on a walk, their response to situations and environments (i.e the park vs a busy pavement) is in part, dictated by your actions, and also your energy that is being transferred through the lead.

Confidence, reassurance, and a strong upbeat attitude in your body language and lead handling when approaching situations, for example - a noisy building site, barking dogs, or simply a busy park helps your dog to feel more confident and reassured in potentially scary situations.

In short, a positive energy will radiate confident energy through your dog.

Chapter Twenty Eight

A New Routine

We are now 2 months into life after Albert and life is very different in so many ways.

Leo had to be treated for 'depression' after weeks of no sleep and chewing off one of his claws. He has been as lost us, constantly searching for him, and not understanding where his pal has gone.

My own grief has amplified his own feelings and knowing this has been tough. If I could have turned off my sadness, I would have, without hesitation but grief is a process that you have to go through.

He has always been by my side and this hasn't changed although it feels different, as if he is the one worrying about me and checking that I am ok. He now sleeps outside our bedroom door. We have tried dog beds but he is having none of it. He just wants to be as close as possible.

My anxious feelings whilst walking him are currently at an all-time high. I am still struggling with the fear that has reared its ugly head from the dog attack, coupled with my overwhelming fear of losing Leo. Throw in a need to avoid people and you have quite a cocktail of emotions, thoughts and barriers to the outside world. So, right now, our walks are shorter, mostly on the lead and far from enjoyable. That is the absolute best that I can do and feeling guilty about it will only serve to reinforce how thoroughly horrible it all is. I choose to believe that it will get easier.

We have talked about getting another dog. At first I was adamant that this was not going to happen (sound familiar?) because the thought of having a different dog in our home was a betrayal to Albert. How could I possibly love another dog like I loved him? Now I feel that Leo would absolutely benefit from having a companion. I am leaving it open for now as our needs are very specific – I cannot entertain the idea of a puppy and Leo is twelve so maybe a senior dog could work for all of us. I am putting no pressure on us and am instead choosing to trust that the right dog will come along if it is meant to be. I did wonder if this book would end with another chapter, welcoming a new dog into our home. For now, this is where the story ends.

Thank you so much for purchasing the book.

Photo Gallery

Leo's First Walk

Albert's First Walk

Partners in Crime

Our Happy Place

Final Note of Gratitude

Kayla,

If you hadn't persevered we would never have had the privilege to love Leo and Albert. If you had listened to me we would never have experienced all the joy and the laughter that these dogs have brought us. If you had not stayed strong and true to your convictions, our lives would have been very, very different and this book would never have been written.

I thank you from the bottom of my heart.

XXX

Contact information

louisegreenauthor@gmail.com

Facebook
https://www.facebook.com/lessonsinpug.co.uk

Instagram
https://www.instagram.com/lessonsinpug

https://www.facebook.com/HattyshoundsPetcare/posts/1702900526525491

https://www.facebook.com/search/top?q=bubblebecca%20pugs

Check out my social media pages and website for videos and more pics of Leo and Albert.

Be the Person

your PUG

thinks you are

Chapters: